NEW FRONTIERS IN EXHIBITION DESIGN

PETER FENG

First Printing: 2014

ISBN-13: 978-1494800963

ISBN-10: 1494800969

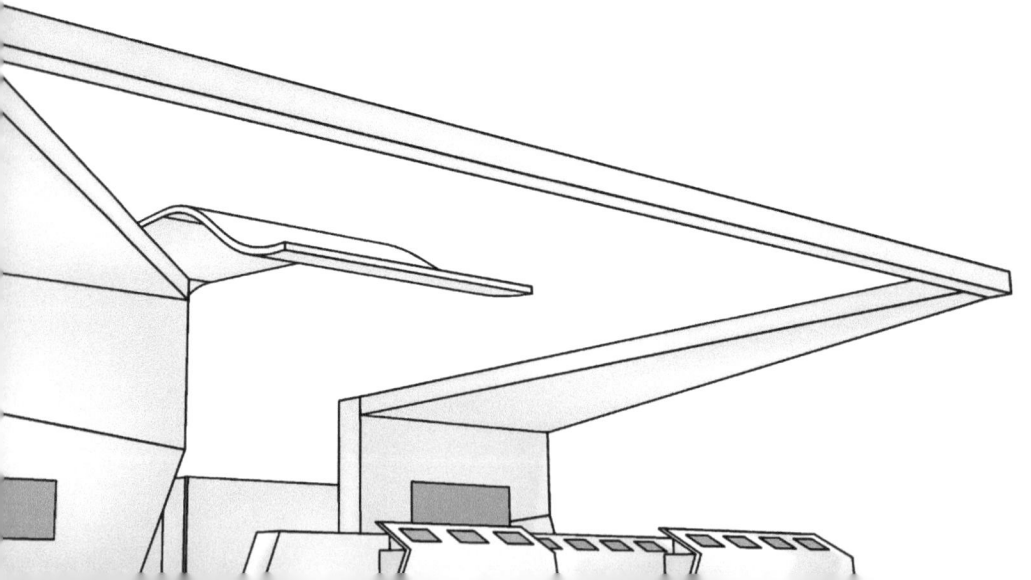

Contents

BlackBerry
@
CTIA 2008

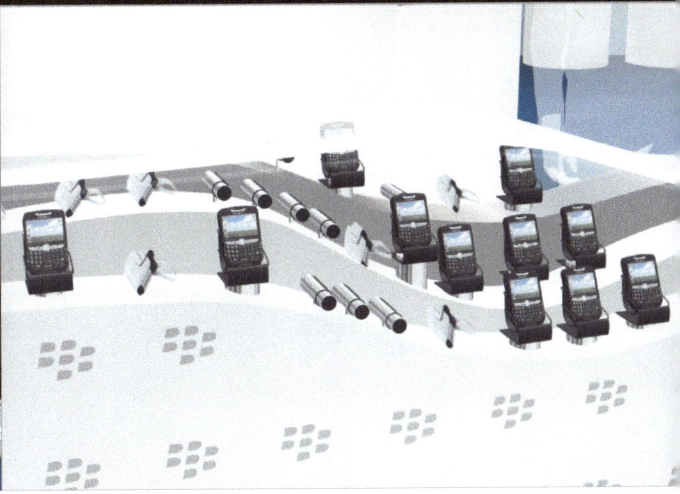

SONY Trade Show Program 2013

SONY Trade Show Program 2013

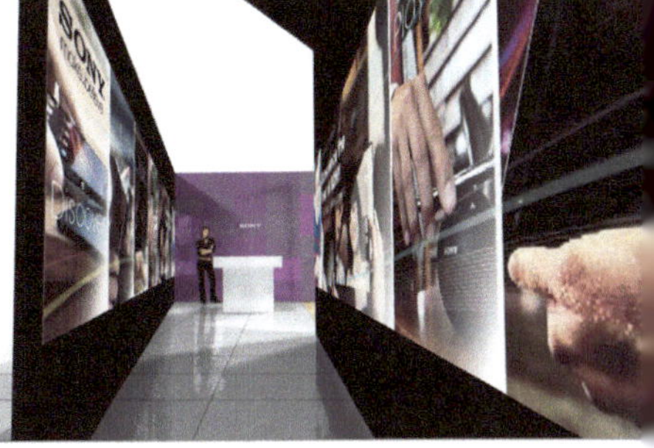

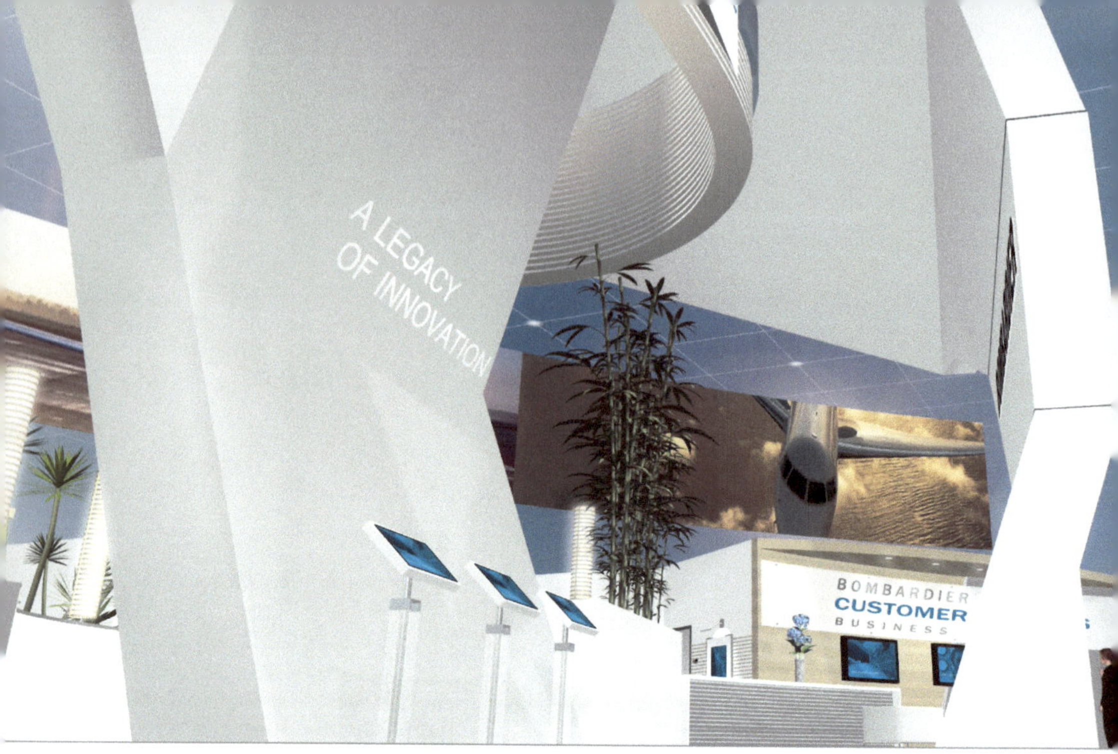

BOMBARDIER @ NBAA 2007

BOMBARDIER
GLOBAL
BOMBARDIER
CHALLENGER

BOMBARDIER
A LEGACY OF INNOVATION
BOMBARDIER
LEARJET
BOMBARDIER
CHALLENGER
BOMBARDIER
GLOBAL
BOMBARDIER
CUSTOMER SERVICES
BUSINESS AIRCRAFT

A LEGACY OF INNOVATION
BOMBARDIER
CHALLENGER
A SOLID INVESTMENT TOOL
THE HIGH-ALTITUDE BOARDROOM
BOMBARDIER
GLOBAL
THE CONSUMMATE BUSINESS JET

Canada Pavilion @ Vancouver Winter Olympics 2010

Future Pavilion - Part 4 @ Shanghai World Expo 2010

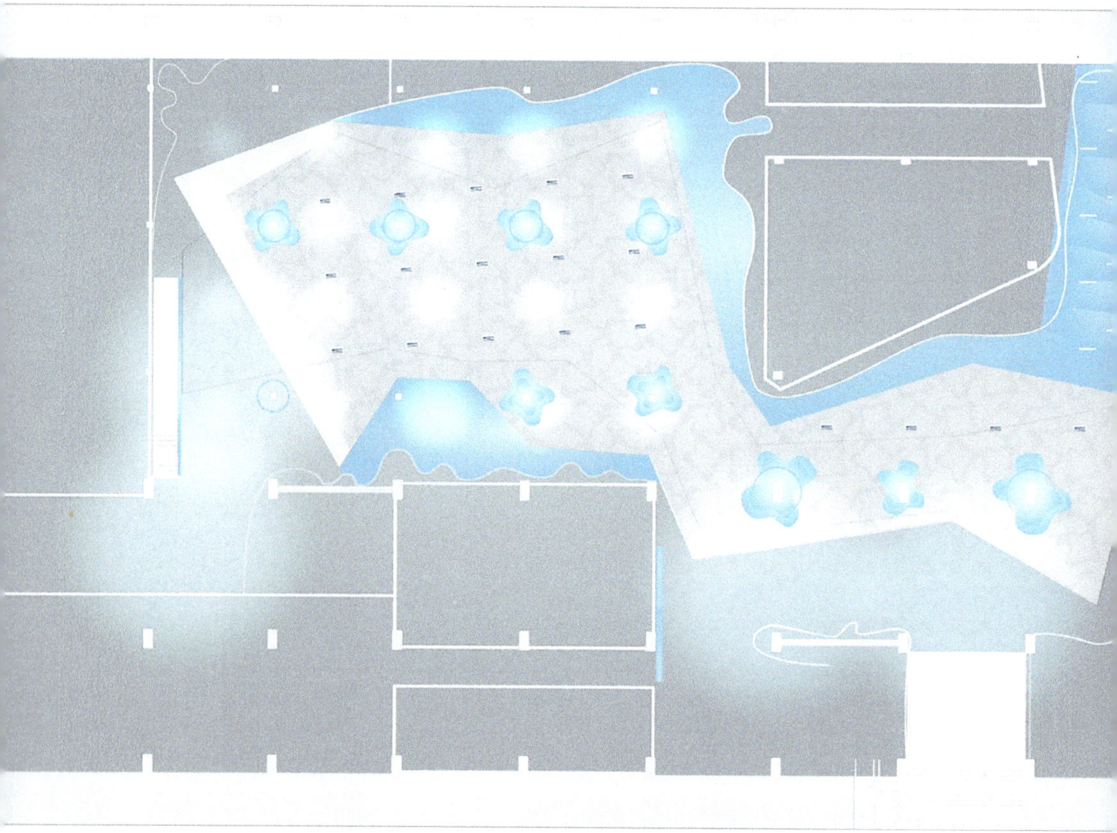

LG @ CES 2009

LG
@
CES
2009

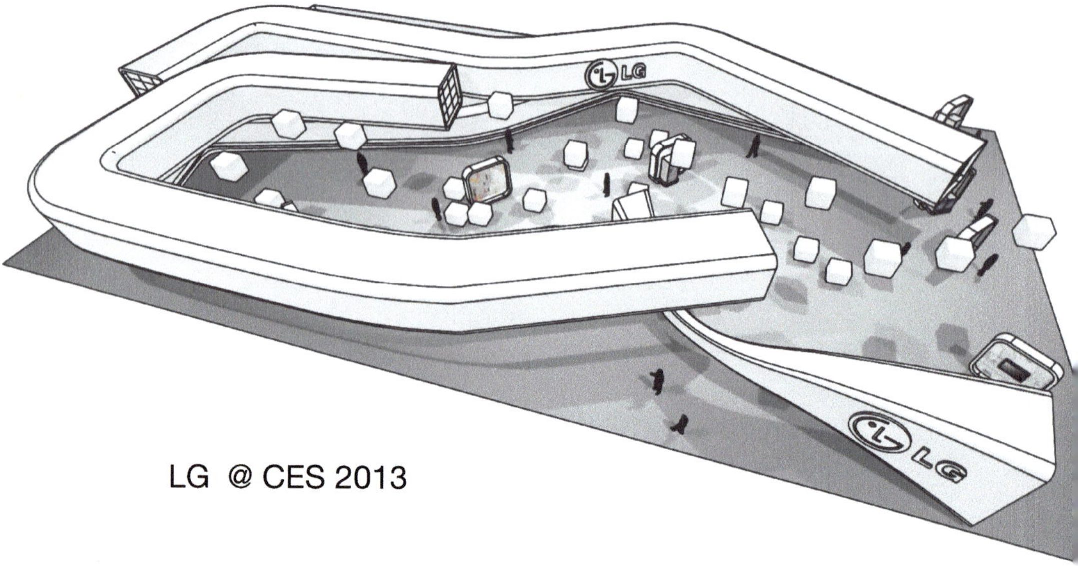

LG @ CES 2013

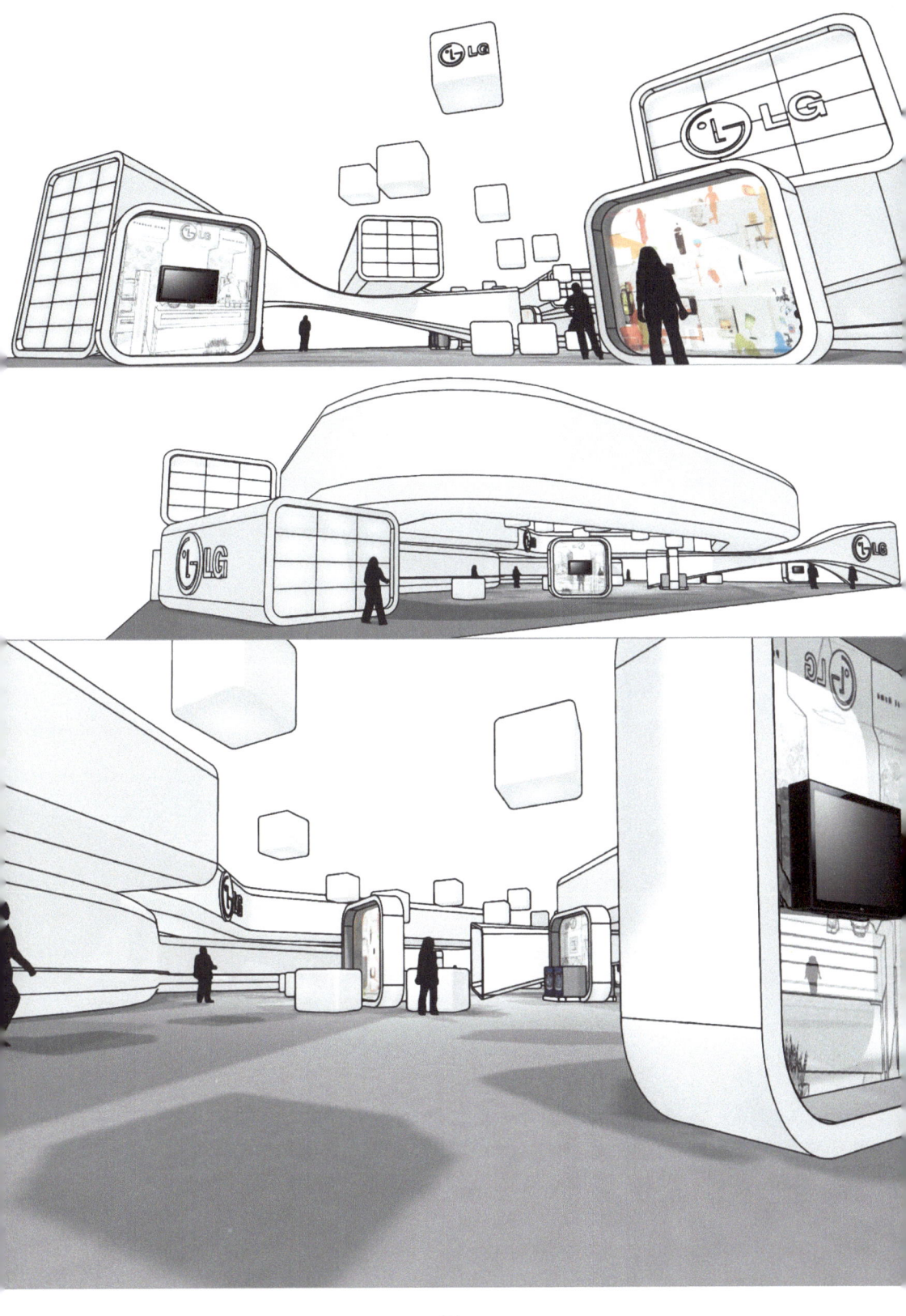

TOYOTA @ Toronto Auto Show 2012

VOLKSWAGEN @ Shanghai Auto Show 2011

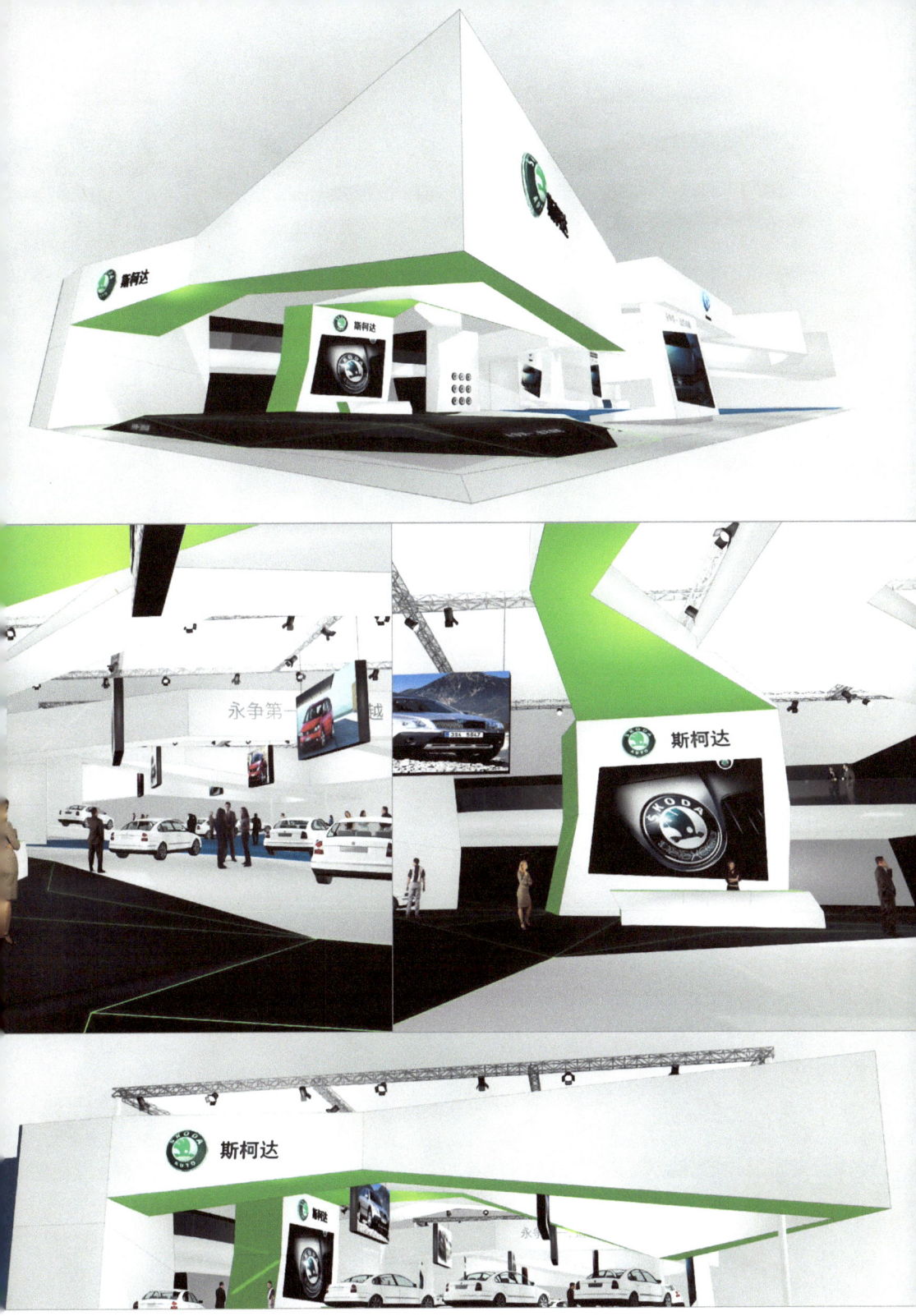

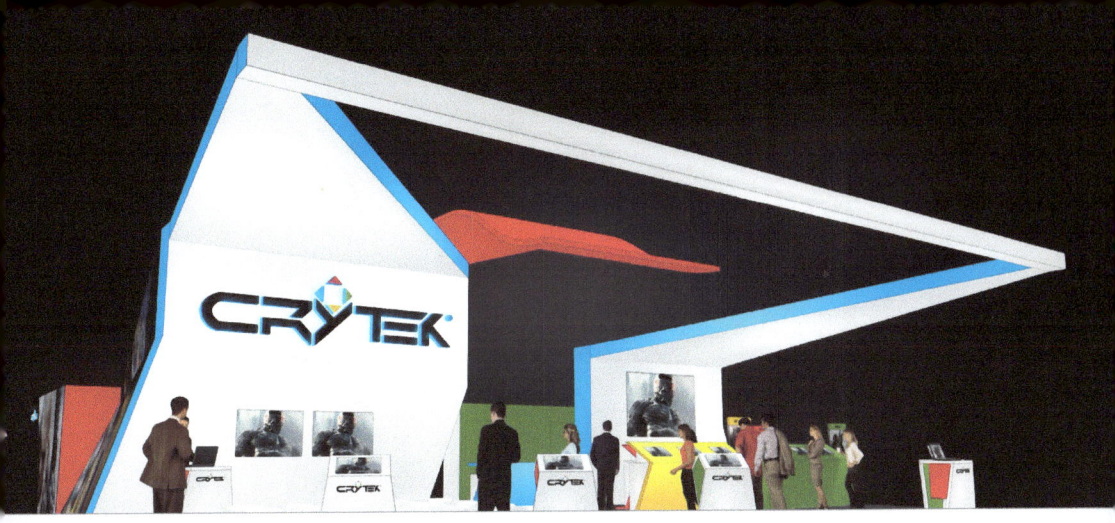

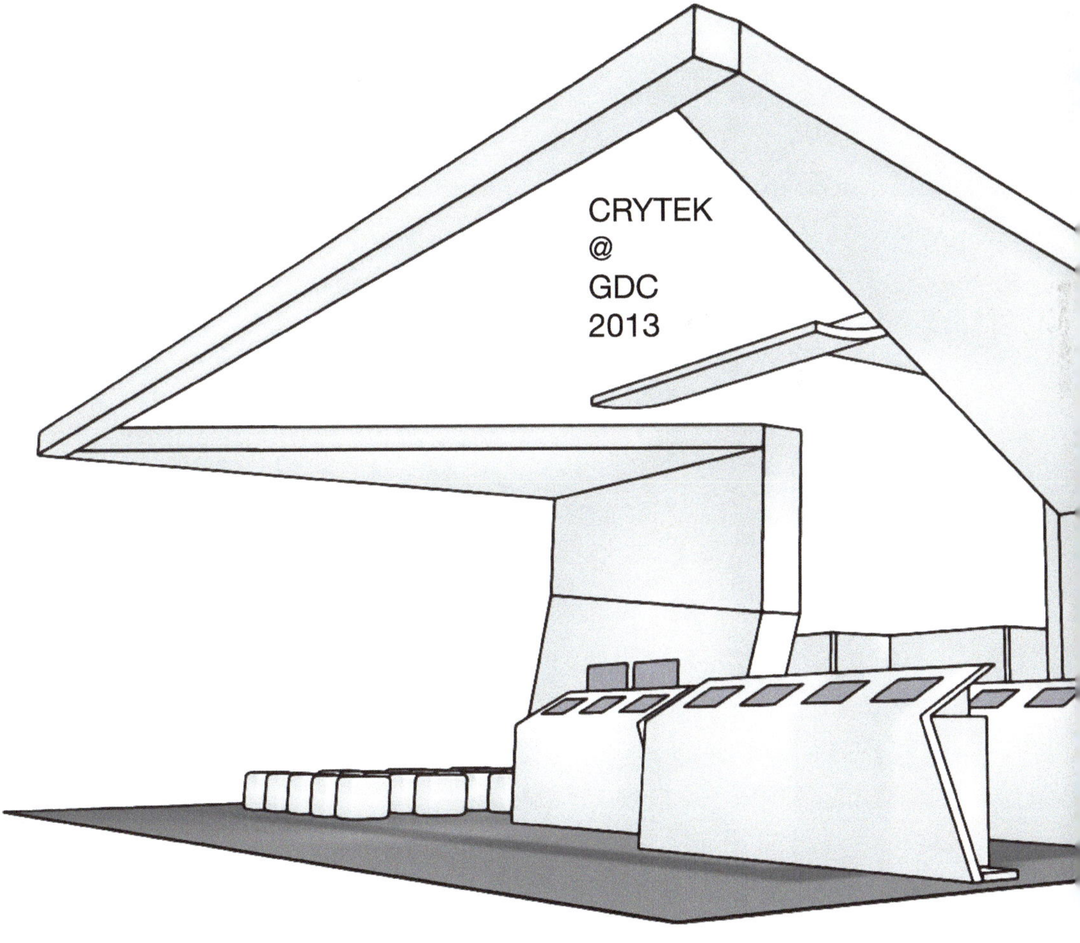

CRYTEK
@
GDC
2013

GameInsight @ GDC 2014

neatfreak @ Chicago Housewares Show 2013

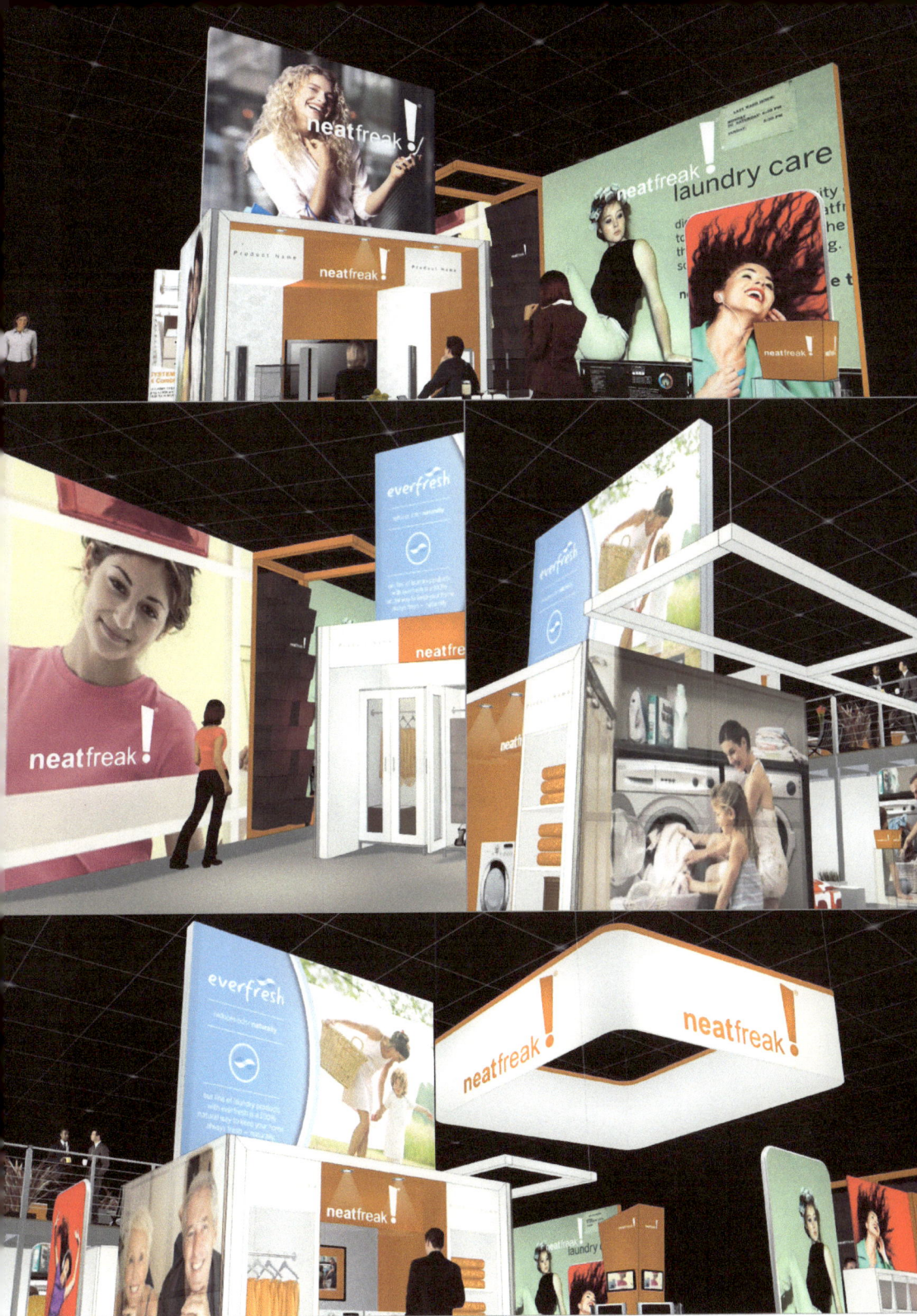

GE Honda
Aero Engine
@
NBAA
2013

GTA @ Toronto Auto Show 2013

PS4 Product Launch Event 2013

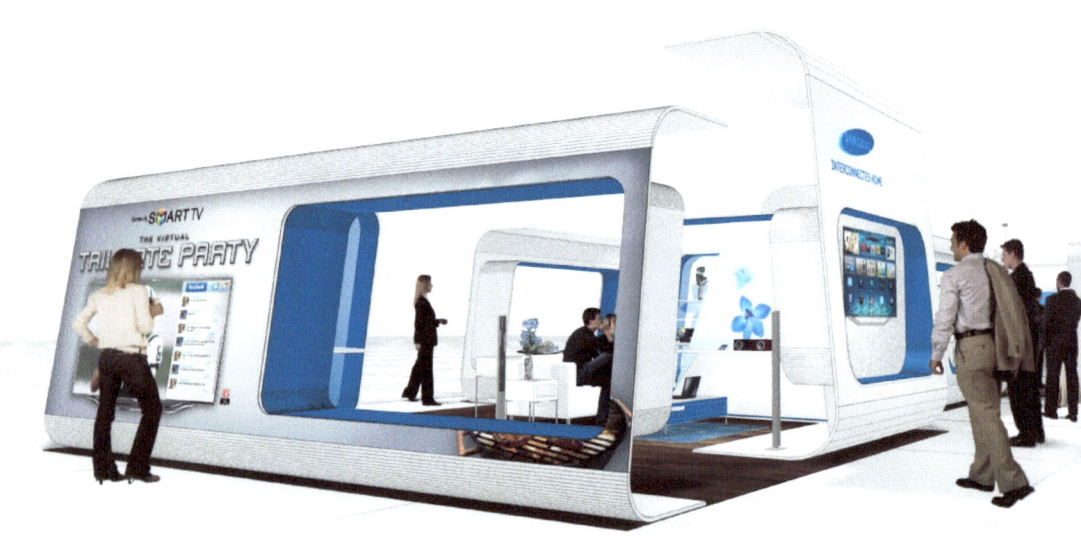

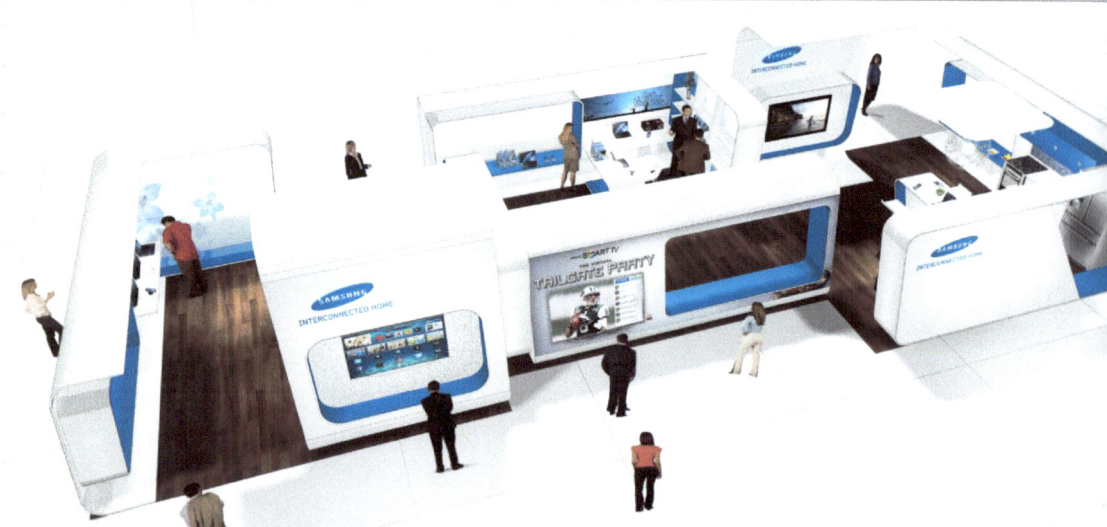

SAMSUNG
Mall
Event
2013

About the Author

I hope I am the sailor in the crow's nest looking beyond the horizon, the sailor who never gives up exploring and searching for a new continent.

I started exhibition design in 1991 immediately after graduating with a bachelor's degree in architecture from the Beijing University of Civil Engineering and Architecture.

In 1995, I moved to Singapore and worked with PICO ART International. In 2002, I immigrated to Canada, continuing my exhibition design career with MICE Canada (An UK public event company which went bankrupt in 2007). In 2007, I started my own design studio — Potato Secret. I have designed exhibits for some famous brands including: Bombardier, Blackberry, LG, SONY, Toyota, Volkswagen, GE, Samsung, and more.

My creative solutions are powered by the emotional perception of client's cooperate culture and product. I truly believe that the inspiration exists inside every client. We just need to unveil it.

Long ago, people asked Michelangelo how he created DAVID, he answered:

"When I passed a quarry, I noticed a huge stone. I looked at the stone and saw David in it. I chipped away the excess, and then everyone saw what I saw."

It sounds so simple — just chip away the excess . . .
        Study your object . . .
                Find your "David" in it . . .
                        and chip away the excess . . .

If we could look beyond the horizon, we would see that there is always a new "David" waiting for us to chip away the excess . . .

peterf1@potatosecret.com

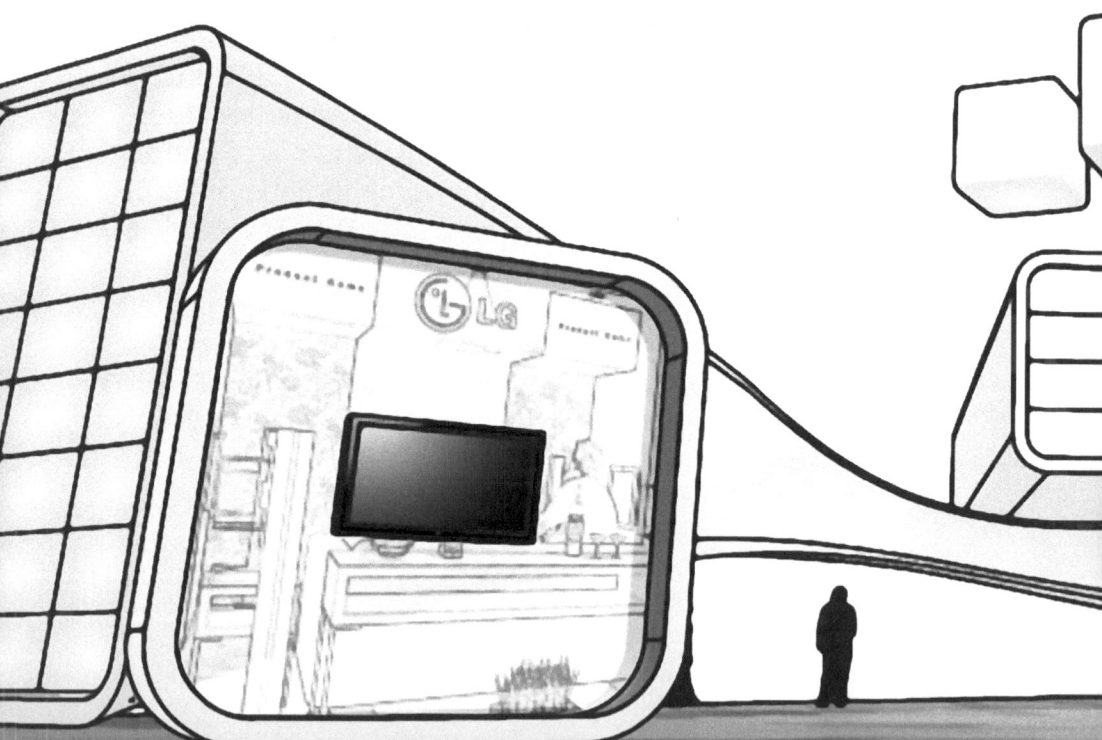

www.ingramcontent.com/pod-product-compliance
Lightning Source LLC
Chambersburg PA
CBHW050755290526
45792CB00008B/2197